NORTH AMERICAN WILDLIFE

WHITE-TAILED DEER

by Joanne Mattern

Kaleidoscope
Minneapolis, MN

The Quest for Discovery Never Ends

....

This edition first published in 2024 by Kaleidoscope Publishing, Inc.

No part of this publication may be reproduced in whole or in part without written permission of the publisher.

For information regarding permission, write to
Kaleidoscope Publishing, Inc.
6012 Blue Circle Drive
Minnetonka, MN 55343

Library of Congress Control Number
2023937043

ISBN
978-1-64519-732-4 (library bound)
978-1-64519-780-5 (ebook)

Text copyright © 2024 by Kaleidoscope Publishing, Inc. All-Star Sports, Bigfoot Books, and associated logos are trademarks and/or registered trademarks of Kaleidoscope Publishing, Inc.

Printed in the United States of America.

FIND ME IF YOU CAN!

Bigfoot lurks within one of the images in this book. It's up to you to find him!

TABLE OF CONTENTS

Chapter 1: Deer on the Run **4**

Chapter 2: A Deer's Body **10**

Chapter 3: Raising a Family **16**

Chapter 4: Deer and People **22**

Beyond the Book *28*
Research Ninja *29*
Further Resources *30*
Glossary *31*
About the Author *32*
Index *32*
Photo Credits *32*

Chapter 1

DEER ON THE RUN

The Sun is beginning to set. A **herd** of deer moves through the forest. They walk slowly through the trees. Sometimes they stop to nibble on a bush or the leaves on a tree.

The deer come to a field. There is plenty of food here for them. The deer **graze** on the grass. They stand with their heads bent down to eat. A few deer lie down in the last patches of Sun. A few others walk slowly. They look into the trees. They are checking for danger.

Suddenly, one of the deer looks around. It sees danger in the trees. A pack of wolves creeps through the forest. They are trying to sneak up on the deer. But the deer has spotted them.

The deer flips its tail up. The white fur underneath looks like a flag. The other deer see it. They stop eating. They freeze in place. The wolves come closer. It's time to run!

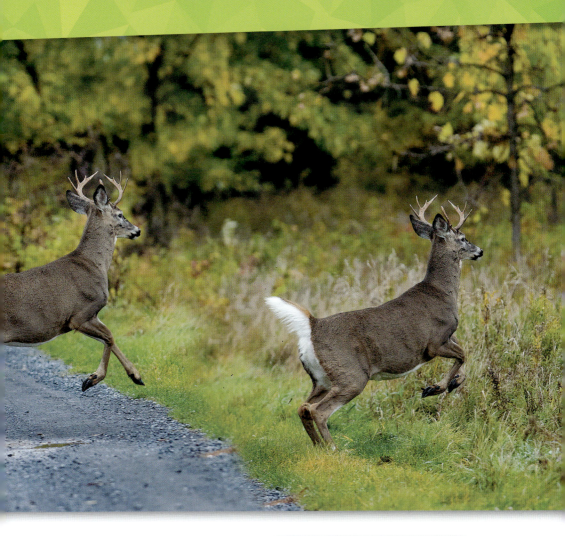

The herd of deer leaps into action. They race across the field. They head toward the safety of the trees. The wolves burst out of the forest. They chase the herd. Who will win?

A white-tailed deer can run more than 30 miles (48 km) per hour!

The deer's path is blocked by a huge fallen tree. But the deer do not stop. Instead, they leap over the tree trunk with room to spare. The deer twist and turn as they reach the trees. Soon they leave the wolves far behind.

White-tailed deer have many **predators** in the forest. These animals are always on the lookout for trouble. They use their speed to get away.

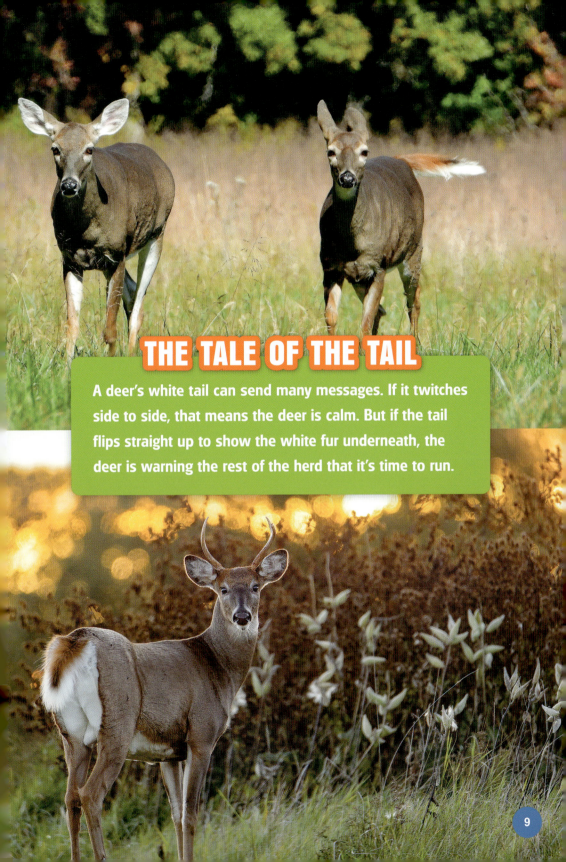

THE TALE OF THE TAIL

A deer's white tail can send many messages. If it twitches side to side, that means the deer is calm. But if the tail flips straight up to show the white fur underneath, the deer is warning the rest of the herd that it's time to run.

Chapter 2

A DEER'S BODY

There are many different **species** of deer. The white-tailed deer is one of the smallest species of deer in North America. But these animals are still quite big. A male deer can be 42 inches (107 cm) tall at the shoulder. He can weigh up to 200 pounds (91 kg). Female deer are a little smaller.

A white-tailed deer's fur changes color depending on the season. In the winter, its coat is grayish brown. In the summer, it is reddish brown. The deer has white fur on its chest and belly.

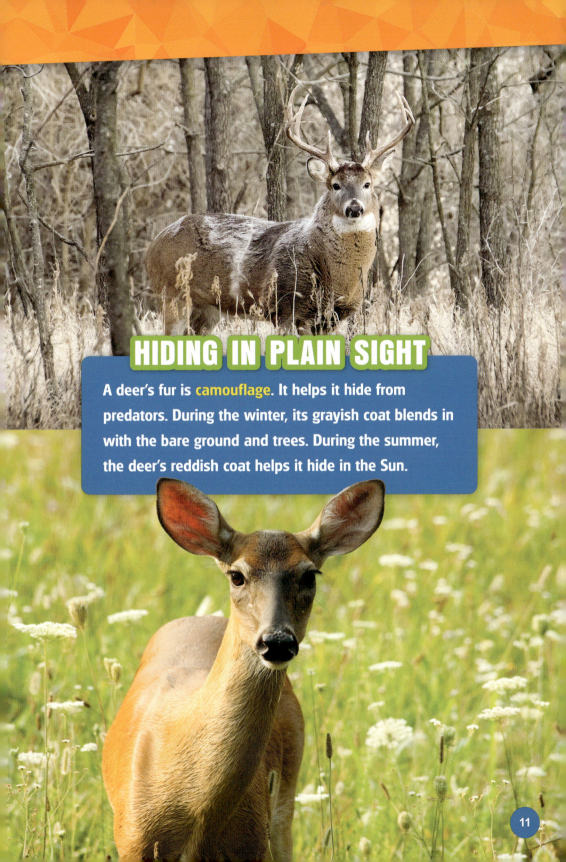

HIDING IN PLAIN SIGHT

A deer's fur is camouflage. It helps it hide from predators. During the winter, its grayish coat blends in with the bare ground and trees. During the summer, the deer's reddish coat helps it hide in the Sun.

Male deer are called bucks. Female deer are called does. It's easy to tell male and female deer apart. Male deer have antlers. Bucks grow antlers in the spring. Antlers grow quickly. Some antlers grow one inch (2.5 cm) per day!

During the spring and summer, antlers are covered with a soft tissue called velvet. In time, the velvet gets hard. The deer will rub it off on a tree or rock to reveal the antlers underneath. Antlers fall off in the winter. The buck will grow a new pair in the spring.

Deer don't use their antlers to protect themselves. They use them to fight with other bucks.

FUN FACT
Rodents and other small animals like to eat shed antlers.

A deer's stomach is very different than ours. Deer are **herbivores**. They eat only plants. Plants are very hard to break down. But a deer's stomach is built to do the job!

A deer's stomach has four parts. The first part is called the rumen. It stores food. When a deer eats, it swallows its food without chewing it. A deer can fill its rumen in just an hour or two. Later, it will push the food back into its mouth and chew it.

The other three parts of the stomach break down the food. Finally, the deer poops out its waste. Deer poop looks like small, black balls.

Chapter 3

RAISING A FAMILY

Male deer live by themselves. During the winter, they chase female deer to **mate** with them. The female gives birth to one or two babies in the spring. Baby deer are called fawns.

Mothers often hide their fawns in the grass while they go to find food.

Fawns have reddish-brown coats. They are covered with white spots. These spots help the fawn hide in the long grass. Fawns stay with their mother for about one year. At first, the mother nurses them. Later, the fawns will eat grass and plants alongside their mother.

Female deer and their fawns often stay together in herds. They feed at dawn and dusk. During the day and night, they lie down in safe spaces under bushes or trees.

When deer are not resting, they are looking for something to eat. Just about any plant tastes good to a deer. These animals eat more than 600 kinds of plants! Grass, leaves, and twigs are all part of a deer's diet. So are acorns, mushrooms, and fruit.

White-tailed deer are usually shy. They are always looking for predators and other dangers. They have a great sense of hearing and smell to alert them of danger. White-tailed deer also have good eyesight. But they can see better in the dark than in the light.

Deer live in many different **habitats**. They live in fields, forests, and swamps all over North America. They live near people in farms, towns, and cities. Any place with lots of plants and open space is a good home for a deer.

Deer are big animals, and they are hunted by big predators. Wolves, coyotes, and bobcats hunt these animals. But the biggest danger to deer is people.

SALTY SNACKS

White-tailed deer do not get enough salt in their plant-filled diet. Bucks especially need salt to help their antlers grow. They seek out salt and other minerals in the earth. Sometimes people put out big blocks of salt for the deer to lick.

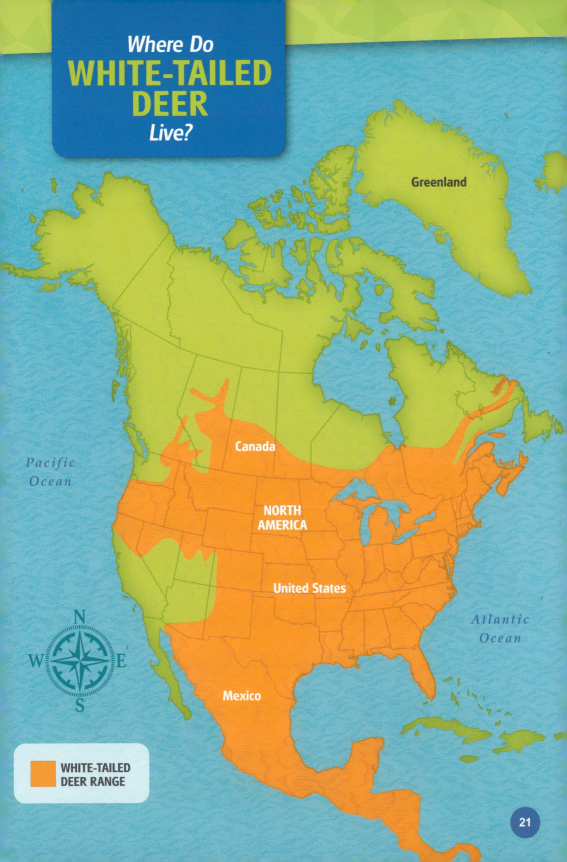

Chapter 4

DEER AND PEOPLE

As more and more forests are cut down, deer move closer to people. Deer are often seen in parks or on golf courses. They roam through neighborhoods. They eat and sleep in people's backyards.

Deer and people do not always get along. Many deer are hit by cars as they cross busy streets. These accidents can kill or seriously injure both deer and people. It's important to look out for deer when driving, especially at dawn and dusk.

Deer can also be pests. They eat food out of people's gardens. They eat crops in farmers' fields.

Some people like having deer around. They feed them. This can be dangerous for both deer and people. The deer might start to depend on people for food. They might also lose their normal fear of people. That can lead to a deer becoming **aggressive**. Deer are big animals with sharp antlers and hooves. They could seriously hurt a person.

Deer also spread disease. Many white-tailed deer carry **parasites**. An insect called a tick often lives on deer. These ticks can spread different diseases. One of the most serious is Lyme disease. This disease is common in the northeastern part of the United States.

Feeding bread to deer can make the animals sick.

In the past, many deer were hunted for sport or for food. This kept the number of deer under control. Deer are still hunted today. But some places are too crowded for hunting. Here, the deer population has become very big. People have to get used to having white-tailed deer as neighbors.

WHERE'S MOM?

Mother deer leave their fawns alone when they are eating. Sometimes people find these fawns and think they have lost their mother. They may take a fawn out of the wild and try to raise it. But the fawn needs to be with its mother. If you find a fawn in the grass or the woods, the best thing to do is leave it alone.

After reading the book, it's time to think about what you learned. Try the following exercises to jump-start your ideas.

THINK

LEARN ABOUT WHITE-TAILED DEER. Deer are very interesting animals. Go to the library or on the Internet to find information about this animal. How long do they live? Which plants are their favorite? Write an article or make a poster featuring fun facts about white-tailed deer.

CREATE

MAKE ANTLERS. Look up pictures of antlers. Then create your own set of antlers out of sticks or paper. Share your work with your family and friends.

SHARE

THE MORE YOU KNOW. Share what you have learned about white-tailed deer with your classmates and friends. What are the main ideas in this book? What makes deer special? Write a report or present a short video to share information.

GROW

HELP A FAWN! Many organizations help fawns and other animals that have been taken from the wild. Find out if there is a wildlife organization in your area. Discuss with your family ways to help these organizations, such as raising money or educating the community about how this group helps white-tailed deer.

RESEARCH NINJA

Visit www.ninjaresearcher.com/7324 to learn how to take your research skills and book report writing to the next level!

Research

DIGITAL LITERACY TOOLS

SEARCH LIKE A PRO
Learn how to use search engines to find useful websites.

FACT OR FAKE
Discover how you can tell a trusted website from an untrustworthy resource.

TEXT DETECTIVE
Explore how to zero in on the information you need most.

SHOW YOUR WORK
Research responsibly—learn how to cite sources.

Write

DOWNLOADABLE BOOK REPORT FORMS

GET TO THE POINT
Learn how to express your main ideas.

PLAN OF ATTACK
Learn prewriting exercises and create an outline.

Further Resources

BOOKS

Albertson, Al. *White-Tailed Deer*. Minneapolis, MN: Bellwether Media, 2020.

McDonald, Amy. *Deer*. Minneapolis, MN: Bellwether Media, 2021.

Statts, Leo. *Deer*. Minneapolis, MN: Abdo Zoom, 2018.

WEBSITES

Factsurfer.com gives you a safe, fun way to find more information.

1. Go to www.factsurfer.com.
2. Enter "White-Tailed Deer" into the search box and click 🔍
3. Select your book cover to see a list of related websites.

Glossary

aggressive: Ready to attack

camouflage: A disguise or natural coloring that allows animals to hide by making them look like their surroundings

graze: To eat grass in a field

habitats: Places where animals or plants are usually found

herbivores: Animals that eat only plants

herd: A large group of animals

mate: To join together to produce babies

parasites: Organisms that get their food from a host animal

predators: Animals that hunt and eat other animals

species: One of the groups into which animals and plants of the same genus are divided

About the Author

Joanne Mattern is the author of hundreds of children's nonfiction books. Her favorite topics include science, animals, sports, history, and biography. Joanne lives in New York State with her husband and family.

Index

aggressive, 24
antlers, 12, 13, 20, 24
bucks, 12, 13, 20
camouflage, 11, 17
colors, 10, 11, 17
dangers, 4, 6, 8, 9, 19, 20, 22, 24
diseases, 24
does, 12, 16
eat, 4, 6, 14, 17, 18, 22, 23, 27
families, 16, 17, 27
fawns, 16, 17, 27
graze, 4
habitats, 20, 22

herbivores, 14
herd, 4, 7, 9, 17
Lyme disease, 24
parasites, 24
predators, 6, 7, 8, 11, 19, 20
range, 21
senses, 19
sizes, 10
stomach, 14
tail, 6, 9
ticks, 24
velvet, 12

PHOTO CREDITS

The images in this book are reproduced through the courtesy of: Dennis W Donohue/Shutterstock Images, cover; James Pierce/Shutterstock Images, p. 3; Ken Schulze/Shutterstock Images, p. 4–5; Mircea Costina/Shutterstock Images, p. 6–7; Jim Cumming/Shutterstock Images, p. 7; Doug McLean/Shutterstock Images, p. 8; Josh0112/Shutterstock Images, p. 9 (top); Aaron J Hill/Shutterstock Images, p. 9 (bottom); Ricardo Reitmeyer/Shutterstock Images, p. 11 (top); G Allen Penton/Shutterstock Images, p. 11 (bottom); Jim Cumming/Shutterstock Images, p. 12; Karel Bock/Shutterstock Images, p. 13; Michael Sean OLeary/Shutterstock Images, p. 14; Aaron J Hill/Shutterstock Images, p. 15; Lester Graham/Shutterstock Images, p. 16; Karel Bock/Shutterstock Images, p. 17; Valerie Johnson/Shutterstock Images, p. 18; K Quinn Ferris/Shutterstock Images, p. 19 (top); BGSmith/Shutterstock Images, p. 19 (bottom); Dennis Adams Creations/Shutterstock Images, p. 20; FocusDzign/Shutterstock Images, p. 22; debra millet/Shutterstock Images, p. 23; Afanasiev Andrii/Shutterstock Images, p. 24 (tick); Tony Campbell/Shutterstock Images, p. 24–25; Steve Oehlenschlager/Shutterstock Images, p. 26; Melinda Fawver/Shutterstock Images, p. 27; James Pierce/Shutterstock Images, p. 31.